the world and the heart

DEDICATION

We would like to acknowledge the support of many people in the preparation of this book, especially that of the Kataññnutā group in Malaysia, Singapore and Australia, for bringing it into production.

the world and the heart

Translated from five discourses given in Thai by

VENERABLE AJAHN ANAN AKIÑCANO

WAT MARP JAN

www.watmarpjan.org

Copyright © 2011 by Wat Marp Jan

ISBN: 978-974-496-740-4

Wat Marp Jan
8/1 Moo 7
Klaeng
Muang
Rayong 21160
Thailand.

Reprinted 10,000 copies in Malaysia, 2012

CONTENTS

PREFACE

"The teachings of the Buddha are always applicable in any time or place," says Ajahn Anan, "but people have to adapt themselves to fit the teachings, not adapt the teachings to fit themselves." Stated in various ways, one can find this assertion throughout Ajahn Anan's talks: *the path exists, it brings results, and we need only to follow it with sincerity.* When talking to his disciples both lay and ordained, Ajahn Anan speaks with wisdom and with abundant goodwill. He repeatedly points them to the Noble Eightfold Path, a path used by the Buddha and countless other enlightened beings over the past 2,500 years.

As a close disciple of the Venerable Ajahn Chah, Ajahn Anan was exposed again and again to the fundamentals of Buddhist practice: kindness and generosity; ethical conduct; developing mindful awareness in all activities; and investigating one's experience in a way that can bring the person to see the *Dhamma*, the Truth. This means seeing through the assorted misunderstandings and false assumptions that we are prone to making about ourselves and the world around us. It means awakening to the natural laws which permeate everything in this world, and in doing so reaching the end of all stress and suffering.

The same themes run gently but persistently through Ajahn Anan's own discourses. Relying on lessons he learned from Ajahn Chah as well as his own experience from nearly 40 years of practice, his talks describe how to correctly integrate the Buddha's teachings into one's life. Having clearly realized for himself the fruits of Buddhist practice, Ajahn Anan now points the way to those who ask. Encouraging people from all walks of life as they proceed along the Path, he emphasizes the same goals: building a reliable foundation within one's heart, and being steady and resilient so as to find "a happiness that doesn't fade."

The World and the Heart is a collection of talks given between 1987-2010 at Wat Marp Jan by Venerable Ajahn Anan Akiñcano. As is customary in the Thai forest tradition, they were delivered spontaneously to the monks and Buddhist lay followers who had come to the monastery to practice the Buddha's teachings. Instructions for practicing mindfulness and meditation are limited in these particular discourses, with greater emphasis placed on developing wisdom and bringing one's life in line with principles of Dhamma. In selecting them, therefore, the translator has assumed that the reader is already familiar with the basics of meditation practice, and perhaps has already begun to integrate the practice into his or her life. If you have never practiced meditation before, that's alright too. There are many teachers and books out there capable of giving basic instructions for concentrating the mind through continuous awareness of an object. One can also find more detailed instructions of meditation methods in *Simple Teachings on Higher Truths*, another compilation of Ajahn Anan's teachings, available for download at www.watmarpjan.org.

Several of Ajahn Anan's loyal disciples were involved in the production of this book, sacrificing their time and energy for the sake of providing an English-speaking audience another opportunity to "listen" to the Dhamma. The translator gratefully acknowledges their invaluable assistance, and takes sole responsibility for any errors contained within. It is my hope that the reader gains as much from contemplating Ajahn Anan's teachings as we have.

May you find a place of refuge in your heart, for it is this that will see you through.

The Translator
March 2011
Rayong, Thailand

Namo Tassa Bhagavato Arahato Sammā-Sambuddhassa
Namo Tassa Bhagavato Arahato Sammā-Sambuddhassa
Namo Tassa Bhagavato Arahato Sammā-Sambuddhassa

THE WORLD
AND THE HEART

Everyone born into this world wishes to be happy. And so people are continually searching and striving for this happiness. It's been like this since we were little. Even before we can speak properly we are already seeking things to satisfy us. As small children we express our wants through gestures, driven by the heart's desires. As we grow up, we work at our studies and acquire as much knowledge as possible so we can get a good job. We assume that having a good job and earning a lot of money will make us happy and at ease.

And yet, even when we have gotten everything there is still discontent. We still don't experience happiness all the time. Various things in the world still cause us to suffer. When we experience gain and good fortune we are happy. But when those things fade away then the heart suffers. At one time we might experience fame or status, but when they disappear the heart suffers. When others praise us we feel happy and content, but when we are criticized the heart suffers. All these worldly conditions—gain, status, praise and pleasure—are uncertain. Sometimes there is loss of gain or status; sometimes we meet with criticism or pain.

This is the way of the world and this is how it has always been. Once born, every one of us receives these things from the world. And when we are all gone and a new generation emerges, it will be like this for them as well. Nothing changes. Even on

New Year's Day, when there is a change of year, this is simply a matter of convention. It's just the way the calendar has been arranged. Arising and passing away is something natural—the sun simply comes into view and goes out of view—but we have prescribed meanings out of it for the sake of mutual agreement and understanding.

Though we are born into this world we fail to see the world. We are entranced by it. We become addicted to the world, that is, addicted to forms, sounds, smells, flavors and tactile sensations. But these things of the world don't last. Arising and ceasing, they undergo change and transformation over time. For this reason the Buddha cautioned his disciples: *Look at this world, beautiful and enticing, like a royal chariot. Those without wisdom are bound by the world. But those who know are not bound.*

The "world" is all the myriad forms, sounds, smells, flavors, and tactile sensations which are desirable and pleasing. The majority of people, if lacking in wisdom, are bound by these things. But the Buddha was no longer bound. So he encouraged his disciples to practice as he had done.

As long as we are residing in the world we must try to cultivate *paññā*, wisdom. Paññā is a brightness appearing in the heart. That all of us have come here shows that our paññā has already begun to appear. By giving up worldly distractions and enjoyments we cut away at the inclination of the heart towards these things. Now instead of going here and there searching for things to entertain us, we have the chance to search for peace. This peace appears as a happiness of heart, a happiness founded in *Dhamma*. At this point we could say that our heart possesses enough wisdom for all of us to see the busyness and confusion in the world. We can see that all those worldly distractions are insubstantial and without meaning.

When we are in a peaceful place though, our mind becomes peaceful as well. It becomes free of stress and agitation, free of doubts and worries, free of scattered thoughts. When we calm our body and speech then our heart will naturally calm down as well, for the heart finds pleasure and contentment in peacefulness. This is called the emergence of wisdom in the heart.

We have this opportunity for training the heart and mind. Our mind is something quite difficult to train, though. As we are sitting with our eyes closed, various thoughts and speculations arise. So we must come to learn about our mind. Why isn't it peaceful? We are looking for peace, looking for the mind to settle down and be still. So why won't it be still? It is simply because we have never trained it. For decades we have let our mind do as it will—ten, twenty, thirty, forty, fifty years; we've never taken the time to train the mind. We've "trained" it in thinking—building up thoughts about this and that—aiming to gain understanding in this way. But each time we reinforce our thoughts and feelings in a worldly manner, our heart gets farther and farther away from peace. As we continue to seek the world to greater degrees, we become increasingly more distant from the Dhamma.

These days people are searching for happiness out in the world more than ever before. People are becoming gradually more scattered and distracted as their hearts drift farther and farther away from the Dhamma. One can see how much busier and hectic the world is these days. In the past when one needed to travel anywhere, there was no rushing or competing. People mostly walked and the paths were wide open. Whether traveling through the forests or through the mountains there was lots of space. But now the world has developed. The roads are more developed. One can travel more quickly than ever before. And so humans find themselves competing with one another. Everyone needs to use the same overcrowded roads because we all depend on vehicles to convey us from one place to another. Wherever one goes there is racing and contending. Although the world is more developed, there is more scrambling and competing than in the past. Things are more convenient, though our hearts are less contented and at ease.

Wherever one finds progress one also finds degeneration. Like in Bangkok. There has been great progress and advancement. However going anywhere is a hassle because there are so many people, and this is simply for the reason that people want to live in a developed place. One can see that progress in the world is inseparable from degeneration in the world. The Pāli word *loka* means "world," and also means "darkness." Along with the growth of darkness comes the appearance of degeneration. This same principle applies to our heart. If our heart develops in worldly ways this means there will be degeneration in our heart. The heart's radiance diminishes as it drifts farther away from the Dhamma.

It is hard to find the opportunity to listen to the Dhamma and practice meditation anymore. We find that in the past people would head for the monastery to perform charitable deeds, seeking tranquility of mind. Because back then there was time and opportunities available to do this. It used to be that the days off here in Thailand were aligned with the lunar observance days[1]. But as things have modernized this has changed to Saturday and Sunday. People's lives are getting steadily more distant from Dhamma.

More than ever before, people nowadays seek for distraction in forms, sounds, smells, flavors and tactile sensations.

These things cover over our heart, deceiving and intoxicating us. But those of us who are able to recognize the danger in allowing ourselves to become agitated and confused can make the effort to practice meditation. This will bring calm and energy to our mind, empowering it to contend with all the various forms, sounds, smells, and flavors around us. Don't let these things take over the mind. Create the conditions for freedom and independence.

The search for Dhamma is the supreme search. Having been born into this world, we desire to obtain wealth and possessions, to acquire a measure of fame and reputation. But regardless of how much wealth, praise and knowledge we may acquire, still we must age, we must become ill, we must die. We must all be separated from this world. Everyone. Without exception.

The sage, therefore—the wise person—will endeavor to reach the Dhamma. He or she will seek the heart's true happiness. For although one might have an education and a career, why is our heart not at peace? When we are insulted, why is it that the heart suffers? When someone criticizes us, why is it that the heart suffers? When our wealth decreases, why is it that the heart suffers? With loss of status, why is it that the heart suffers? When the body experiences change or transformation, why is it that the heart suffers? It is simply because our heart is not yet endowed with wisdom.

If you have already progressed far enough in your career and have an adequate amount of wealth, then you should consider seeking the Dhamma within your heart. Let us bring wisdom to our heart, so that we can understand the things of this world in line with truth.

When we are first born everything is unfamiliar and one is swept up in the world. Having never contemplated the process that is our life, we don't understand the reality of it. Our lives don't last long. Once born, we have around 100 years at most. Those who live longer than this are rare. And as for our desires, what could we possibly desire from this world when the time comes to leave it behind? But if there is still greed, anger and delusion remaining at the time of death, our consciousness will seek birth in another womb. It will be born into the world again and then swept up by the world again. It will be striving and struggling again. We will have to go back to school and study all over again and then go seeking again. Every birth, every life, with no end to it.

Each birth, each life is bound up with *dukkha*, suffering. The heart experiences nothing but dukkha. Because whenever we don't get what we wish for then we experience dukkha; or when the body changes in some way or we develop an illness we experience dukkha. Searching for the four necessities—food, clothing, shelter and medicine—is also dukkha. The fact that we have to go to a job, being vulnerable to the moods of our superiors is dukkha; or if we are the one in a position of authority and get irritated with our employees, this is also dukkha. All of these forms of dukkha come about, are made possible, simply by the fact that we have been born into the world. And as long as we delight in the sensual pleasures of the world, we must be born and die, again and again, on and on indefinitely. The Buddha said that we have been born countless times and experienced great suffering and despair from being separated from those things and people which we are fond of. The amount of tears we have shed is more than all the water in the great oceans, He said. Birth brings with it a great deal of grief and pain.

The Buddha attained to the state of awakening within his heart. But in order to give rise to awakening within—a heart which is radiant, free of anger and hostility—we must make the effort to practice. Keep on investigating the heart and you will become one who is heedful. Here is a practice for all of you to undertake from now on: if there is suffering present for whatever reason, then we need to try and remedy that suffering to remove it from the heart.

Even in a worldly way, every person wishes to be endowed with mindfulness and wisdom. If we are truly wise though, then we will come to understand the fundamental nature of *sankhāras*, compounded phenomena. They are *anicca*, *dukkha* and *anattā*—impermanent, unsatisfactory and not-self. If we have the wisdom necessary to see the reality of compounded phenomena, suffering will diminish. But the wisdom which will arise in the heart is something we must seek for ourselves. We must study and practice the teachings for ourselves. No matter how much money one might have there isn't anyone we can buy this wisdom from, unlike external possessions which we are able to shop for and purchase.

Internal possessions are something we have to acquire on our own. We have to do it ourself, bringing this wisdom into existence and making our heart bright. For this reason we should endeavor to develop *pāramī* (spiritual maturity) within ourselves. You have all travelled here to Wat Marp Jan. While we are here practicing meditation there is peacefulness in our speech and actions. Our minds are established in morality and we are restrained and careful. We can say that we are practicing giving in the sense that we are giving up other distractions to come to the monastery.

The path of giving, morality and meditation has the ability to lead anyone's heart to a state of radiance and peace. This is the path that will lead us to see the *saccadhamma*, the Truth, which always exists in the world. No longer fooled by the world—no longer being excessively caught up in sights, sounds, smells, flavors and tactile sensations—we can come to understand the reality of conditioned things.

That the world is plagued by disharmony and confusion is due to the presence of craving, a craving which is never appeased. We can let craving take us outside the boundaries of virtuous conduct or we can choose to carry out our life within these boundaries. Once we have established ourselves within the boundaries of virtuous conduct, we must begin to investigate the three kinds of craving in order to understand them. There is *kāma taṇhā*, which means finding satisfaction and delight in sense objects—sights, sounds, smells, flavors, tactile sensations and ideas. Then there is *bhava taṇhā*, craving for being or for experiencing, and *vibhava taṇhā*, craving for not-being or not-experiencing. *Kāma taṇhā, bhava taṇhā, vibhava taṇhā*—these are the causes for the arising of stress and suffering. If we don't practice we will never be able to see these conditions of the mind as they actually are.

Practicing the Dhamma is for the purpose of bringing the mind to see and understand—to see the world in line with truth. If we truly see the world this means we have seen the Dhamma. The external world is one thing, and the internal world is just this body and the moods in our heart which are continually arising and changing. We may feel anger or attraction or aversion or stress: the moods and emotions that arise in the heart are of all sorts. During the course of one day there is endless arising and ceasing. If we see the nature of these thoughts and feelings as they arise and cease this means that we see the world. The mind will temporarily distance itself from these mental phenomena. When we regularly see our thoughts as impermanent, as unsatisfactory, as not-self, the mind will stop grabbing onto them. We'll be able to separate them from one another, just like water and oil. This is how one can see the true nature of the world.

When the heart comes to understand reality, one will experience great rapture and happiness. How much happiness will there be in the heart? To whatever degree one can realize Truth, the heart will be bright and spacious and will experience that degree of happiness. If the heart attains to an even greater degree of calm and concentration—genuine *samādhi* with rapture appearing nearly all throughout the day and night— well, experience it for yourself and you'll know what that level of happiness is like. This is a kind of happiness that doesn't depend on wealth or possessions. It's a happiness independent of sights, independent of sounds, independent of smells, independent of flavors, independent of sensations and independent of ideas—a happiness coming from within.

To whatever extent humans seek for happiness outside themselves, the farther they are away from the happiness within. But those who make the effort to seek the happiness of the heart can find a happiness that doesn't fade. It's for this reason that all of you should seek the Dhamma.

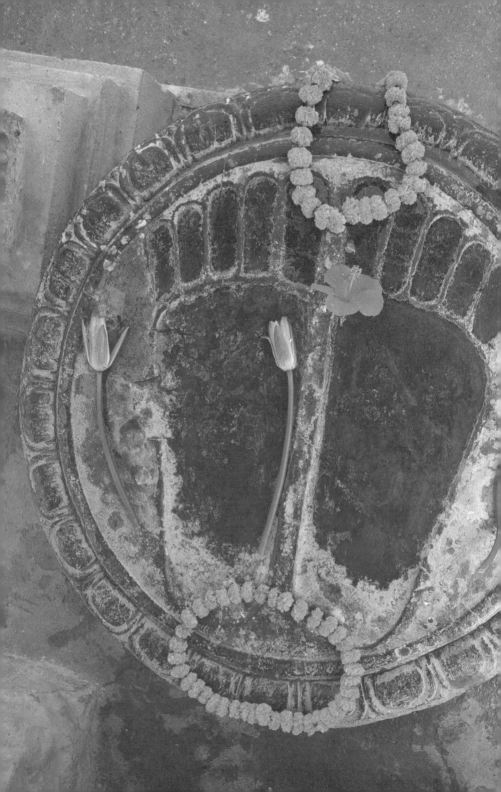

FINDING THE PATH

We are all interested in bringing about that which is good and beneficial. This is what is meant by "merit." Merit (*puñña*) is that which lifts up the heart, that which fills the heart with goodness. The opposite of merit is wrongdoing (*pāpa*), synonymous with heat.

It's nearly Māgha Pūjā, the day the Buddha delivered the *Ovādapāṭimokkha*[2] sermon and said,

Sabbapāpassa akaraṇaṁ:
Refraining from all wrongdoing.
Kusalassūpasampadā:
Bringing goodness to perfection.
Sacitta-pariyodapanaṁ:
Making the mind pure and unblemished.
Etaṁ Buddhāna sāsanaṁ:
These three principles are the teachings of all Buddhas.

The great number of Buddhas who have already come and gone all expounded the Ovādapāṭimokkha just as our Buddha did. And the next Buddha to arise in the world will proclaim this same teaching. It won't be any different. In their essence, the Buddha's teachings can be summarized as abandoning the unwholesome, cultivating the wholesome, and purifying the mind. This is the heart of Buddhism. Or we could look at these three directives as being like the three main arteries that run through our hearts.

THE HEART'S BASIS

When we come to practice, we must dispel that which is damaging from our hearts as much as we can. We both abandon wrongdoing and incline towards goodness as well. Sometimes it's the case that people will perform wholesome deeds but haven't given up other deeds which are unwholesome. Although they do things which are good, the bad hasn't been given up yet. In the beginning, just focus on two things: speech and actions. Start by gradually reducing unskillful ways of speaking and acting, and then move onto making your words and deeds beneficial.

As for making the mind pure, this is accomplished through developing wisdom. Investigating and then letting go of matters of body and mind—this is what's meant by making the mind pure. When we incline towards goodness through building pāramī, doing charitable deeds and so on, this is merit. As for wrongdoing, today we have come here to do good acts and so aren't committing any wrongdoing through speech or action. This is *sīla*, moral discipline, and we could say that this sīla is what protects and nurtures all other wholesome qualities.

Even though as lay practitioners we may have a lot of duties, if we are resolute in our practice we won't be heedless. Anything that is wrong we give up. We start by abstaining from killing, abstaining from stealing, abstaining from sexual misconduct, abstaining from lying, and abstaining from intoxicants. Look, we've all made mistakes in the past, but from now on we're going to keep to these five precepts. If we habitually maintain the five precepts, then when we fix our mindfulness on the in-and-out breath or on the word *Buddho*[3], our meditation practice will bring us peace.

It's important that we understand what is meant by meditation practice. The Buddha taught for us to develop our *kammaṭṭhāna*. "Kamma" means work; "ṭhāna," a basis. In other words, we need to work on a firm basis for the heart. Because the nature of the heart is that it's constantly in motion. When the heart is moving here and there following thoughts and moods, there is no stillness. Without stillness we can't see the truth.

Therefore, we have to train the heart to be still. Sometimes we are able to concentrate the mind, sometimes not, sometimes we feel agitated and confused. Please try to endure through it, though, for this is part of our discipline. *Khantī paramaṁ tapo tītikkhā*: Patient endurance is the supreme incinerator of defilement. So we ground ourselves in this next principle of the Ovādapāṭimokkha discourse as well, relying on patience and endurance to burn up the mental defilements (*kilesa*). When we are established in moral discipline, even if we are criticized or insulted we don't retaliate or respond in kind. It's not because we lack wit or intelligence—we have plenty of the sort of intelligence which goes in the way of defilement. But we don't respond because we give importance to our sīla. This moral discipline is what will look after us.

Right here we're already close to *Nibbāna*, close to seeing the Dhamma in any moment. Because we're walking the Noble Path[4]. We're in line with Right Speech, Right Action and Right Livelihood; that is to say, we're established in morality. When our morality is firm then we have Right View. We incline towards acting in ways that are wholesome and meritorious, which is Right Intention. We have the intention to refrain from cruelty or ill-will, whether through body, speech or mind. We incline towards goodness and that which is beneficial for ourself and others. At this point our heart is on the Path.

WALKING THE CORRECT PATH

When we have the wisdom necessary to see the harm of being without moral discipline and the benefit of being with moral discipline, then we make the effort to keep practicing. It's not enough to stop at this point; even if it's difficult we need to add to the meritorious karma we have already made. Cultivating the four *brahmavihāras* (sublime abidings) is an important meditation practice. There is *mettā*, goodwill for others; *karuṇā*, thoughts of wanting to help those who are suffering; *muditā*, feeling gladness and appreciation for the goodness in other people; and *upekkhā*, equanimity in situations when we are not able to help. These four brahmavihāras will care for our heart, protecting it from sadness and depression. This is a meditation theme which can help to make our practice of concentration strong and stable.

Really work at concentrating the mind. You can try to make it one with this single word "Bud-dho," for when the mind is truly with *Buddho*, it is utterly still and peaceful. There is no longer any fear in the heart. One can go and stay in frightening places like cremation grounds[5], and upon recollecting *Buddho* the heart will become brave and courageous. Piles of bones scattered about are nothing special. We've got bones as well. The only difference is that ours can still speak and eat and walk around. *This* body hasn't died yet. It hasn't been overcome by disease yet. *This* body is still hanging in there. But one day it will have to break down, which means we're all in exactly the same boat. When we contemplate the impermanence, unsatisfactoriness and not-self of the body, we will see that there is nothing to it. Everyone who is born must die.

Since the Buddha has clearly shown the way, what's left is for us to practice. And our practice must be grounded in the principles of morality, concentration (*samādhi*) and wisdom[6]. There are no other principles, no other path which can lead us to see the Dhamma. It is only through cultivating the Noble Eightfold Path, the Buddha said, that realizing one of the four stages of enlightenment[7] is possible: *Just as there are no tracks in the sky, there are no enlightened beings outside of the Noble Eightfold Path.*

The path of morality, concentration and wisdom is something important. One can't just do things any old way. Solely watching the mind, for example. If this practice isn't joined with a basis of concentration, wisdom won't come about. There's just not enough strength of mind. Perhaps one is able to observe the mind as it proliferates—one can see the arising, enduring and ceasing—but there's not enough strength and stillness of mind to eliminate the mental defilements. We need to bring the mind to a state of calm so as to gather the energy to investigate. This is the proper method.

Say we're practicing meditation in a peaceful place and watching leaves falling off the trees. If our mind is still, as we watch the leaves falling to the ground, it can appear to us as like the lives of human beings falling away, leading us back to the truth of the body and bringing about genuine insight. The mind may then unify in concentration, giving rise to *tadaṅga-vimutti*, a temporary liberation of the mind through wisdom. And if the power of our mind reaches a greater level still, it is even possible to attain to perfect clarity of insight right at that moment.

SHAPING OUR FUTURE

In India at the time of the Buddha there were two dominant beliefs: that after death one is annihilated; and that whatever level one has been born at in this life, one will forever continue to be born at that level of existence[8]. But that's not how it works. The heart takes rebirth according to our karma, repeatedly cycling through *saṁsāra* in various forms of existence. And because our various births are dictated by our karma, if we create bad karma the heart will accordingly take birth in a lower form of existence where one finds only suffering and torment.

Therefore the heart is the important thing. All forms of karma are performed in our actions, in our speech, or in our thoughts. When we create virtuous karma we will be happy. This is because our heart is not harming itself or others. It is abiding in goodness. And at the time of death, a heart that is pure and established in goodness will go to heaven, the Buddha said. A heart that is afflicted, on the other hand, will go to hell. This is dependent on the state of the heart at the moment the body dies.

The fact that a Buddha can arise in the world, that one can realize enlightenment, cannot have come about by just being born in this lifetime only. The Buddha wasn't just suddenly able to attain enlightenment as the foremost in the world, greater than all humans, heavenly beings, and gods within the three-world system[9]. That's not how it happened. In order to become the Fully-Enlightened Buddha, He had to perfect the ten pāramīs over countless lifetimes, much more than other human beings. This was so that in His final birth He could reach enlightenment with a heart greater than any other in any realm. It's not the case that He was able to become the Buddha without ever having developed Himself previously. That's not how it was.

Yet whether people believe in rebirth or not, if they consistently make bad karma through body, speech and mind, they will meet with suffering right here in the present because their hearts are afflicted. Others may not see their pain, but they themselves will know. And if there is rebirth, these people will meet with even greater pain and suffering.

On the other hand, those who believe that one is not annihilated at the time of death, that we will be reborn according to our karma—these people will try to live their lives skillfully in the present. Doing good, abandoning evil, making the mind bright—if there is life after death then people who conduct themselves in this way will meet with comfort. And even if there isn't they will still experience happiness in the present.

With regard to our beliefs, some things we cannot prove. At times we must rely on faith instead. There is faith in the Great Teacher who was enlightened over 2500 years ago along with the ability to recollect His previous births and the ability to know the future. The teachings of the Buddha are flawless. Heavens, hells, brahma realms[10] and Nibbāna definitely exist. These are facts which the Buddha proclaimed on the basis of His knowledges of previous births and the disappearing and reappearing of beings according to their karma. He saw absolutely clearly that death is followed by rebirth, as opposed to annihilation.

These days, however, people educate themselves to a high degree based on scientific principles. They seek to understand cause and effect within the present moment. In order to believe in something they must be able to prove it. If that's the case, then they can look to the present for proof. When one acts in good ways, creating skillful karma, then there is happiness. When we don't harm others, isn't it good? When everyone is established in morality then there is harmony and happiness. We have thoughts free from cruelty and animosity, developing goodwill for one another. The result is happiness and ease; our hearts are joyful. But if someone nurtures vengefulness and ill-will—what effect is that going to have? There will only be gloominess and depression.

Either way, look at the present. Heavens, hells, brahma realms or Nibbāna: we can look for these right now in our own heart. There's nowhere else we need to look.

When Ajahn Chah went to practice under Luang Pu Kinaree[11] he once came upon a large number of red and black ants battling one another. Ajahn Chah sat there watching, cheering on the opposing sides. Sometimes he cheered for the red ants and sometimes he cheered for the black ants. Luang Pu Kinaree walked up and said, "Oh! Up to heaven. Oh! Down to hell." And then he walked away. He taught like a Zen master, in a way that made one think.

So Ajahn Chah considered, *Ehh, how could one go between heaven and hell that easily?* He had a lot of mental tranquility already, so when he reflected on this it became crystal clear: *Ohh, it lies with the heart. This very heart here. Happiness and suffering equal heaven and hell right here in the present.*

If one isn't yet grounded in morality then the heart is at the level of a lower being. But later on, having adopted moral standards, the heart rises to the level of a true human being. But if the heart is without morality then it can drop down. Now that we've met with the Buddha's teachings, we should work to lead the heart to a higher birth. If we have to take rebirth, let it at least be an improved birth. And it's right here in the present that this work is done.

VIEWING THE WORLD WITH WISDOM

We've all taken birth into this world. So we develop the understanding that the body is "us" and all the things we can acquire are "ours." The house, the car—it all belongs to us. But when these things are lost, stolen, or simply wear out, then suffering appears in our heart. This is because we have attached to these things as ours. This is the cause. This doesn't mean we are negligent with our possessions; we still have to look after them so that they can be used for a long time. But we make use of them with mindfulness and wisdom, reminding ourselves, *These things are impermanent, alright? They don't really belong to me.*

Ajahn Chah was constantly reminding the monks and laypeople to keep their mindfulness on guard. Can you see? All the material things in our possession must be consistently reflected upon. *One day the glass will break, alright? The car has to break down, alright?* This is called using our things with wisdom. This is different from making use of things blindly.

We like new things. We think that anything new must be better. This is the way that ignorance, craving and attachment[12] fool us. But look, even if we acquire something new it goes and gets old just the same. We're always seeking things outside of us because it's not difficult to do. But why don't we make time for seeking our heart? Why don't we work to renew our heart?

One more year passes by and our body undergoes one more year of degeneration. Do we see this happening? Or do we only see the things that we've acquired? Sometimes we have to look at what has been lost. One more year of our time in this world has gone; our time remaining has decreased. In regard to this the Buddha has us frequently reflect: *The days and nights are relentlessly passing by; how well am I spending my time?*

Our lives are not far from death. We must bring up this recollection of death sometimes, such as asking ourselves what we want from this life. What would be of real substance? We may want wealth, status, praise and pleasure. But one day these things will leave us. We can seek them, but they cannot last forever.

This body of ours which we're so fond of—our parents look after it until we're grown. They give it food and water, getting medicine for it when it's sick and finding it a place to stay. But this body doesn't follow our wishes. It simply goes its own way according to causes and conditions. In the end it has to fall apart because this is how bodies are.

As practitioners we must be interested in following the ways of Dhamma and cultivating our minds. Because what our minds need is calm and stillness. We tell the mind to be at peace, so why isn't it peaceful? We don't want any thoughts of hostility and bitterness towards others—*stop right now!* we tell it—but it doesn't stop. If delusion, craving and attachment are weakened, though, then the mind can be made to stop. For this reason we must train our mind. *A mind that is well-trained brings happiness*, the Buddha said.

STEPS TOWARDS LIBERATION

When one first starts out there may be various doubts about the practice of Dhamma. Is it really effective? What is *jhāna* (mental absorption) like? What is *magga-phala*[13] like? *What's the quickest way to get results?* There may be a lot of uncertainty. So one goes searching for answers in things outside oneself. One goes looking around for a path of practice. One looks around for a teacher. But later on, when we've found conviction in the

Buddha, Dhamma and Sangha, our commitment to the practice will come from within.

When I was looking for a teacher, I ended up ordaining at Wat Nong Pah Pong[14] to live with Ajahn Chah. He didn't teach all that much—he just taught us to be mindful. He told us to keep the mind from becoming pleased or displeased throughout the day. This is important. The mind is stirred up when it meets with moods, becoming pleased or displeased, so we need steady mindfulness to keep up with these reactions of the mind.

When we have started practicing meditation, combined with a foundation of moral integrity this will help bring greater peace to our mind. If you have a lot of work and duties then cultivate mindfulness in the midst of that work. And to whatever extent is possible, make time for chanting and meditation each day to help calm the mind. When we put more time into the practice—making it continuous, something we do every day—our meditation will improve.

After practicing like this for some time, one day the mind will become sufficiently still. When the mind has reached a suitable degree of calm, this is when our contemplation can produce the insight that the body is transient, is stressful and is not-self. The teachings of the Buddha will then become clear. And even if we don't realize the Dhamma in this life, the fruits of our effort will still carry into our next life. As for those that are able to get results in this life, this is a reflection of their past practice and accumulated merit.

You don't need to wonder about how much merit you've already accumulated, though. If you believe in the Buddha's teachings—either by faith or by insight—just keep practicing. Wherever you go, try to keep the word "Bud-dho" with you at all times to supervise the heart. This is important. For when the heart merges with *Bud-dho* (or *Dham-mo* or *San-gho*), we become the true *Buddho*—"the one who knows, the one who is awake, the one who is joyful"—and are capable of understanding the Buddha's teachings without difficulty.

Whether we reach Nibbāna in this life or not, we just keep building up our pāramīs until we come to see the Dhamma with total clarity. So please train yourselves well in ways of body, speech and mind. Wherever you go, don't forget *Buddho* or the practice of contemplation, for these are our means to bring peace to the heart. Keep investigating until you can see that all compounded phenomena—both material and mental—are impermanent, unsatisfactory and not-self. Right here is where the path which leads beyond suffering is found.

This path—the *ariyamagga*—is a most important vehicle. *Ariya* means "that which is supreme." *Magga* means path. So it's the supreme path, the supreme vehicle, greater than any other vehicle in the world. No matter what vehicle we might find to take us out of this physical world, we still wouldn't escape from the endless cycles of birth and death in saṁsāra. Thus we need to rely on the vehicle of the Noble Path, for this is the most important vehicle there is. May you all progress in Dhamma.

FROM WISDOM,
FREEDOM

One should regularly consider the fact that everything in this world is impermanent. Our bodies are impermanent and so we can't avoid dying. Set up mindfulness and reflect on this again and again. As we come to accept and trust in this natural law—the law of Truth—suffering will begin to diminish.

Ajahn Chah would use the simile of watching a log floating downstream. It travels with the current, eventually ending up in the ocean. But if we wish for the current to flow back the way it has already come…this just isn't possible. That's the way of nature. We look to see the truth in nature, that all the things of this world are impermanent, unsatisfactory and not-self. When the new ordination hall at Wat Nong Pah Pong developed cracks in the cement, a layman came to inform Ajahn Chah. "That's right!" he told the layman. "If the hall didn't crack like this there wouldn't have been a Buddha! You see?" he continued. "These things are impermanent. It's just natural—no matter how well-built, they change according to causes and conditions."

Like with our new hall here at Wat Marp Jan. We've tried to build it to be strong and long lasting. And yet the properties it is composed of are already degenerating, breaking apart every moment. This is the way of nature, of compounded things. Having come together, they then begin to break apart.

The body comes into existence, made up of the four elemental properties of earth, water, fire and air. Once it has come together and we are born, from that point on it is gradually breaking down. But we think it's growing up. A child grows from one month to two months…eight months…nine months… one year…two years, steadily growing up. And our parents are so happy to see this. Once we reach a certain age, though, the signs of degeneration are clearly visible. But actually the body has been degenerating from the time we were born. This is the nature of compounded things, including the bodily formation.

Still, the mind attaches to the whole lot of it as being ours. This is called trying to take possession of nature. We take the body as belonging to us, but we need to realize that this is only true on the conventional level. We can say it's us, but it's only a convention. For in actuality this is not correct. This bodily formation belongs to us only in the sense that we think of it that way. The truth is that we merely depend on these properties of nature for a certain period of time. Please reflect on this. This is the way to take the heart beyond attachment, arriving at a place of freedom.

Desire and aversion, dullness, restlessness and doubt— these mental hindrances are the conditions which prevent goodness from arising and the mind from becoming calm. Have you ever noticed? We sit down to practice meditation, intending to keep the mind with the breath and *Buddho*, and then it flies off into thinking and proliferation, going to forms, sounds, smells, tastes and sensations which we find pleasing. Or else we think of something upsetting and the opposite appears: anger, vengefulness and agitation. Sometimes we're filled with doubts or feel frustrated over a range of unimportant issues. You see? These things just suddenly appear. Sometimes when sitting meditation we can experience incredible sleepiness. This is the hindrance of dullness enveloping the mind.

When we come to meditate we discover the state of our mind: constantly oppressed by the mental hindrances. So we have to practice. We have to concentrate the mind in order to free it from the hindrances for a period of time. This is called suppressing the defilements. One then investigates to see the lack of core in everything around us, to see that this body is merely elements, not a person or self. When we see all the things of this world as impermanent, unsatisfactory and not-self, the heart will be able to reach a temporary freedom from suffering.

Try to investigate regularly in this way. Regularly work at concentrating the mind. Firmly establish yourself in moral discipline as a normal way of life. This is the foundation. Although concentration and wisdom may not have yet appeared, please keep yourselves grounded in sīla. We need to be patient.

Sometimes we get anger arising. The eye sees a form: *This guy again!* and suddenly we're furious. The heart is hot as fire, being burned by the defilements. *I'm not going to take this. I don't let anyone treat me this way and I'm not giving in to you!* In the past when we got angry, there was no attempt to control our speech or actions. It was, "Alright then!" and we might start throwing things or even physically attack someone. But as Dhamma practitioners we don't accept this way anymore.

When anger arises we simply endure it patiently. We may want to hurt the other person, to use harsh, cutting, sarcastic speech. But instead we just endure; we restrain our impulses, using morality as our basis. The defilements would have us shout at the other person, would have us respond and set them straight. But as we are intent on caring for our moral discipline, we just patiently endure. If we don't have a sense of morality around these things, our words will be coarse and uncivil. So we just have to train ourselves, ok?

It's normal for people to get angry like this before they've started to practice, but it's something we have to work with. Some people, however, have dispositions that tend strongly towards anger. For these people working with the anger is more difficult. If you find anger arising a lot, then take mettā (loving kindness) or the brahmavihāras as your regular meditation theme. Develop peacefulness of heart through the practice of mettā. We can bring up thoughts of goodwill directed firstly towards ourself, reciting the verse, "May I be happy; may I be free from suffering." We then spread these thoughts of goodwill to include all beings: "May they all be happy and free from suffering." This is a skillful means for calming the mind. In the beginning we wear down the defilements with patient endurance. Then when we are able to keep with our meditation theme, the mind will fall under our control and become cool. See? This is practice.

When we first come to train the mind, the anger can be quite strong and there is still a lot of attachment. But after practicing for just a little while, we will already be able to observe a decrease in the intensity of our anger and we won't stay angry long. This is progress. Eventually, when moral discipline, concentration and wisdom mature and gather together, we'll be able to see that all things are simply conventions (samutti). The "monks" are conventions, "men" and "women" are conventions; on the ultimate level there is no core behind these labels. There is only impermanence, unsatisfactoriness and selflessness. When we can see that nothing of this world is able to last or endure, this is wisdom. When wisdom arises, freedom from suffering (vimutti) arises in the heart.

But the natural tendency of the mind is to attach to all of its moods. This is the process of ignorance, craving and attachment, leading to becoming and birth. In other words, it is the cause for the arising of suffering. In awakening to the Dhamma, the Buddha found that all suffering which arises in the heart arises dependent on causes. It doesn't just appear out of nowhere.

For instance, when we meet with things that are unwished for, suffering arises. When we don't obtain something we wish for, suffering arises. When we forget the fact that separation from the things that we like is inevitable, suffering arises. And this suffering is a Noble Truth, a natural consequence of a mind that still has ignorance, craving and attachment.

The Buddha discovered that the causes and conditions which bring about suffering are part of a process. This is the underlying principle of dependent origination: *when this exists, there is the arising of that.* In other words, when the process begins with fundamental ignorance, it leads on to craving and attachment and gives rise to suffering[15]. At this point the Buddha was able to find the cessation of suffering (*nirodha*) and the method of practice which brings it about.

The Noble Truth of Cessation means the shedding of craving, the casting off and relinquishment of all mental defilements, the extinguishing of suffering. This is the release from all attachment. There is no longer any place in the heart for craving to reside. And if there is no residence for craving, suffering simply cannot arise. This is the way of causes and conditions.

The Buddha found the way to make the heart open and spacious, free from suffering. This is cessation. So we need to develop the Noble Eightfold Path—the direct path. It begins with Right View, a view that brings benefit. Then there is Right Intention, Right Speech, Right Action, Right Livelihood, Right Effort, Right Mindfulness and Right Concentration. These are the ways of wisdom, morality and concentration.

Concentration means making the mind firmly settled on a single object. One can use the meditation word *Buddho*, for example, or the breath, or if one is skilled in cultivating mettā meditation, then one can practice along those lines. These are skillful means for making the mind calm. For if we are going to develop wisdom in order to see the conventional reality of body and mind—that these things are not ours, are not a person or self—then we need to rely on a mind that has been calmed and is established in moral restraint.

Today we can set up the intention to keep the five precepts all throughout the day. Make the resolve for one day and one night. In this way we will become rooted in these five guidelines. If we learn to restrain our actions and speech, it becomes a foundation. Even if concentration is not yet arising, it will. And when it does arise, the concentration that is built on a foundation of morality will be strong and focused. This is stepping onto the Eightfold Path of morality, concentration and wisdom.

When we develop the Path in this way the mind will be firmly concentrated in samādhi. When the mind is well controlled, this is the time to study the body and mind. Contemplate to see the body as simply the body and the mind as simply the mind. It's not a person or a self. This is where wisdom will arise. And when wisdom is arising, there is continuous, uninterrupted mindfulness.

Continuous mindfulness means we know the arising and ceasing of body and mind. When this knowing gathers together it will cut off and eliminate the defilements. From then on there is knowing present in the mind, able to see the arising and ceasing of phenomena. In the beginning, seeing arising and ceasing is the way of walking the path. One carries on in this direction until the path unifies and one arrives at absolute clarity: the insight arises that everything in this world is merely conventions. The mind is then released, freed from all attachment. In order for wisdom and insight to arise, however, the mind must be supported by moral discipline and concentration of mind which is strong and stable.

Concentration doesn't come about easily though. This is because there are things keeping it from arising. The mind is constantly getting carried away in forms, sounds, smells, flavors, tactile sensations and ideas. These are the external sense media (*āyatana*). And then there are the internal sense media: the eyes, ears, nose, tongue, body and mind itself. The moment of contact between them is called *phassa*. And what happens next?

Phassa (contact) is the condition that gives rise to *vedanā* (feeling): pleasant, unpleasant and neither pleasant-nor-unpleasant. But when one of these three feelings arises that's not the end of it. When feeling arises, taṇhā (craving) immediately follows—it's just cause and effect. When we are pleased with something, the mind indulges in it. Indulging in something is called kāma taṇhā, or sensual craving. While we are indulging, if there is desire for the happiness and pleasure to remain, this is bhava taṇhā, the craving for being or experiencing. It is a craving for things to continue and increase. If it happens that something is unpleasant, this will give rise to vibhava taṇhā, the craving for not-being or not-experiencing.

This is how craving is born. At the point of contact— bang!—a feeling arises and then craving arises. The process is extremely fast. And when craving arises, attachment arises along with it. This is the arising of "me" and "mine," my self, my things, my happiness. This is the arising of becoming and birth, of ageing, death, sorrow, lamentation, pain, grief and despair. And the process of dependent origination reaches the end of the sequence.

Once this suffering has appeared, though, the process starts again and travels back in reverse. There is the origination of birth and then of becoming. Attachment occurs, giving rise to craving, and then feeling arises from that. Contact arises next and the process travels all the way back to fundamental ignorance (*avijjā*). Back and forth, back and forth like this. It happens so fast.

What are we to do? Ajahn Chah compared it to falling out of a tree: falling from the tree tops, passing numerous branches on the way down, and then hitting the ground. As we collect ourself, all we know is that we're bruised and in pain, not how many branches we've passed. We may not be able to observe all the factors of the process, but we know that we are suffering.

So we need to be cautious and apply ourselves to the practice. Train the mind to become still. When the mind has been made reasonably still, mindfulness will be able to stay on top of all mental impressions (*ārammaṇa*) that come into our awareness through the six sense doors. One will see that these impressions are just that much, not to be taken as *me* or *mine*. When there is mindfulness there will be wisdom. Attachment won't take place. All moods and mental impressions are seen as anicca, dukkha and anattā, not as a person or a self. The mind won't go and attach. This not-attaching is what we mean by letting go.

This is the point of tadaṅga-vimutti, the temporary liberation of the mind. *Vimutti* means "release." Letting go of all mental impressions, the mind doesn't attach to anything. It is temporarily released from all ignorance, craving and attachment. Liking and disliking will not take place in response to impressions coming in through the sense doors.

Eventually, though, the mind will begin attaching again. As mindfulness weakens, it can't maintain that level of wisdom anymore. There is contact at the eyes, ears, nose, tongue and body, as well as ideas arising from within, and the mind starts attaching again, taking things as *me* and *mine*. Our mindfulness just can't keep up. The causes for suffering then appear once again in the mind.

At this stage the practice will alternate back and forth like this. So we have to develop our mindfulness to be even sharper, even quicker. Whenever anything contacts the mind, we need to be aware of that and investigate. If there is mindfulness, there will also be wisdom. We must stay on top of all mental impressions, knowing them as merely conventional truths. There is no real, lasting self.

This sense of self is born from attachment to the things we come in contact with. So now we have subject and object, "me" and "them." *This person praised me, that person insulted me,* etc. And then there are the various material things which come and go—these we also take as ours.

When we get something and feel pleased: this is kāma taṇhā. Soon it changes to vibhava taṇhā, not wanting things to fall apart or be taken away. Whenever something falls apart it disturbs us and we suffer over it. This is because of vibhava taṇhā, which is a cause for the arising of suffering. See? And on top of this, when this suffering arises we take *it* to be ours as well! When we're really suffering we can't even eat or sleep; the mind is consumed by thinking and agitation. And all of this comes from the sense of self. There is no mindfulness and so wisdom cannot arise.

We need to address this. With regards to our possessions, we can regularly contemplate the impermanence in them, telling ourself, *This is something uncertain, ok? It can't last.* Ajahn Chah used the example of seeing a glass as already broken. When we keep this reflection in mind, then wisdom is already present as we lift it up to drink. Mindfulness is operating from the outset and as we lift the glass there is awareness. Alongside this we recollect the Buddha's teaching of anicca: *Ah, this glass is impermanent. And the one who is using this glass is also impermanent. There's no lasting core in either of these things, ok?*

Contemplate this often. When we regularly contemplate in this way, mindfulness becomes sustained. Moments of wisdom start to link up and form a ring. Mindfulness and wisdom steadily grow, concentration becomes firmer. Our speech and actions are rooted in moral discipline, and moral discipline that is well maintained brings concentration as its reward. When concentration is well developed the fruit of this is wisdom. Wisdom that is well developed brings insight and liberation, meaning the mind no longer experiences suffering. This is all there is to it.

So let's all make the effort to practice. We can use contemplation as a means to bring about one-pointedness of mind. Reflect on the conventional nature of body and mind, that they are things unworthy of attaching to. When there are no people, no us or them, then the heart is at ease, experiencing emptiness.

But don't think that you can achieve this right away by simply doing nothing. Not putting forth effort, not focusing on any meditation object—that doesn't work. First we have to walk the path. We have to practice. We take food into our mouth, chew it up, swallow it, and in the end we feel full. But if we just sit there looking at the food, telling ourself we feel full…this won't bring any benefit. When we walk the path then fullness will come about naturally, the same as if we take food and eat it.

Like these grey-robed Zen monks who traveled to Thailand from Korea. At the time these monks arrived at our monastery I was sitting next to Ajahn Chah as his attendant. He told the lay people, "Ok, everyone bow, these are monks." They probably couldn't tell that these were monks, for the monks here wear an ochre robe. But the Thai people are good: when the master tells them to bow, they bow. Ajahn Chah said, "These are monks, alright? Monks according to conventions. A monk on the ultimate level must arise within the heart. This can occur for a lay practitioner as well."

So these monks from Korea had come to ask Ajahn Chah some questions. "Why do we need to practice?" they asked. "What is the purpose of practice? How should we practice? What result can we expect from practice?"

And Ajahn Chah…oh, his wisdom faculty was *so* sharp. Ajahn Chah's paññā was extremely quick. He didn't take any time to consider it at all—he didn't even *think*. When the question finished the answer came forth *immediately*. And he answered Zen-style. The questioner asked in the Zen manner, so Ajahn Chah became a Zen master.

"Why do we need to eat?" he asked.

Let's all think about this: why do we need to eat? What's it for?

"How do we go about eating?" he continued.

"And once we've eaten, what is the result?"

This is how he answered. And they *understood*.

See, they already understood why we need to practice, how to practice, what the results are said to be—they already knew perfectly well. And yet this knowledge hadn't reached the heart. Their understanding was still quite surface-level; it hadn't yet gone in deep. But when Ajahn Chah gave this answer it went straight to their hearts in a most profound way. *Ohh, so this is how we have to practice. We have to walk the Noble Eightfold Path. And when we've walked it, it will lead us beyond suffering.*

There is suffering in our heart. And there is a cause for this suffering embedded in our heart. These monks from Korea understood this before they came, but the understanding was still on the outside. Now, though, there was knowing within. Rapture, gladness and contentment arose. They told us that they had been asking these questions all over the world but until now they still hadn't found the answer they were looking for. It must have been their accumulated merit that led them to find a teacher like Ajahn Chah, someone who could respond with such wit and profundity.

So we should ask ourselves the same: *Why is it necessary for us to practice? Why should we be moral? Why do we meditate? What is the correct way of practice? And what results can we expect from this?* You can ask these questions yourself. Contemplate them until you find the answers. And when you find the answers this will indicate the arising of wisdom.

SOMETHING THAT ENDURES

C onsider this thing we call *me*, this body—made up of the four elements of earth, water, fire and air. Whatever has the characteristic of hardness, such as bones, hair, nails, teeth, skin—all of this is the earth element. The liquids in the body, the blood: this is the water element. That which helps to digest food and keep the body warm is the fire element. And then there is the air element: the breath going in and out, the winds in the body.

Contemplating on a deeper level, what we have are particles of matter. According to what we have learned from science, there are neutrons, protons and electrons which join together to make a single atom. And when multiple atoms come together, they appear to us as a body. Now if our mind is tranquil and refined we will be able to investigate this. When we are able to divide the elemental properties in this way we will see the emptiness of this body. It is not a being, a person or a self, but simply a conglomeration of elements.

Similarly, all inanimate objects—for example this hall we're sitting in, or a tree, or a mountain—are only particles. Broken down far enough, all there is to be found is emptiness. It is this characteristic of clustering together which obscures seeing the *anattā* in things. Anattā means not-self. When various parts have gathered together and are viewed as a whole, we will see them as *attā*, as a self. This is when the sense of self arises. The Buddha demonstrated this to the five ascetics[16] in the *Anattalakkhaṇa Sutta* (The Discourse on the Characteristic of Not-Self) when he asked:

> "Is this form permanent or impermanent? Feelings, perceptions, mental formations, consciousness[17]: are they stable and lasting? In other words, are they likely to remain forever?"

> "No, Lord," answered the five ascetics. "They are impermanent."

> "And anything that is impermanent, that is subject to change, and that cannot endure is unsatisfactory, right?"

The five ascetics reflected and understood that anything which is subject to continuous change is dukkha. Dukkha means unable to endure. When something is unenduring, it is dukkha. It has instability as its nature and cannot be made otherwise.

The Buddha continued, asking, "so then, form, feelings, perceptions, mental formations and consciousness: can these be taken as a self?" And the five ascetics, led by the Venerable Aññā Koṇḍañña, contemplated this and saw that they are not a self. Because there is nothing there which will obey our commands. There is only arising, existing and ceasing. When we see conventions (*samutti*) as they really are, right here is where the mind will be able to attain to freedom (*vimutti*) from all forms of defilement.

So you see? The essence of the Buddha's teaching is to bring about the arising of wisdom within us. Ajahn Chah taught that that which will give rise to wisdom are just these themes of impermanence, unsatisfactoriness and not-self. We need to investigate those things which we are attaching to as *me* and *myself*, to allow us to see that they are in fact not a self. Form, feelings, perceptions, mental formations and consciousness: we attach to these as *me* or *mine*; as beings, people, or selves; supposing that we are this or that; wanting to be this or that; on and on to no end. But if we can see the self as not a self, it can be said that we have seen the true self[18]. Or this could be called seeing the Dhamma, which is the same as seeing the Buddha.

Some monks who stayed close to the Buddha—even if they were to hold onto His robe—still didn't see the Tathāgata[19], the Buddha said. All they saw was the physical body—the grouping of earth, water, fire and air—but they couldn't see the real Buddha. To see the real Buddha one must see the Dhamma.

As we come to see the Buddha, to see the Truth—the Dhamma—the defilements will decrease naturally. *Sakkāya-diṭṭhi*[20] will be gradually eliminated until our understanding is perfectly clear. The mind can then enter the stream of Nibbāna; that is, one cannot fall back to the lower realms of birth[21]. When the truth is seen, the mind will be beyond the world—*lokuttara*. Yes, there is still some greed, anger and delusion in the mind, but it has more mindfulness than before. One has greater control over the mind than before. Right here is the beginning of true goodness, which all of us monks and lay practitioners can reach through our practice. If our contemplation frequently gives rise to wisdom then it won't be difficult. Do it a lot. Develop it well.

When we put forth the effort to practice, we can make the mind peaceful by contemplating. If we contemplate mental impressions which gain entry at the eyes, ears, nose, tongue, body and mind, we'll see that they are impermanent and uncertain. Or we can contemplate the impermanence and uncertainty of this physical body. It's a collection of transient properties, a collection of dukkha, a collection of anattā. There is no self which can be found there. Using wisdom in this way can lead to samādhi, a state of tranquility.

Once the mind has been calmed, we can investigate again. Profound understanding may then arise, seeing that this body and mind are really not a self. When it has seen the emptiness of all phenomena, the mind will be able to let go. So we keep an eye on the mental impressions which we have seen as impermanent, unsatisfactory and not-self, relating to them without attachment.

In the Zen tradition they teach this with the simile of a window covered in fine particles of dust. Equipped with mindfulness, we apply ourselves to steadily wiping it clean. But later on, by contemplating the window—the mind, that is—we see that there's no self there at all. So we let go completely. If there's no window there is nothing for the dust to attach to. In the same way, when we see that the mind is not "us," what is there for the mental impressions to stick to? It's anattā.

This is how it's done. When we have progressed on the path then we can one day arrive at the core of the Buddha's teachings. So keep practicing. Practice in order to see conventional reality as it actually is.

SEEING CONVENTIONS

Ajahn Chah would often give the following example: we can take a glass and call it *kaew nam* in Thai; in the Pāli language we would refer to it differently; in Chinese, in Hindi, in English it is called something different still. Because actually there is no glass. It's just elements that humans have brought together in a certain way to produce this thing. If the elements are pulled apart again then it isn't there. It's empty. This is what is meant by convention.

But we firmly cling to these things as if they are real. If somebody calls the glass a chamber pot it disturbs us. "Please hand me that chamber pot," someone says and we feel like, *That's not a chamber pot, it's a glass!* But these are only conventions. If we really contemplate these things, the heart will be released. We will realize that until now we had never fully understood the truth.

In reality, there isn't any *thing* there. When we understand the truth, the heart becomes bright and clear. It's as if the heart, fooled by conventions for so long, has been turned upright. It has been liberated from attachment, realizing that all the things of this world, including this body and mind, are without any abiding essence of self. It's just not correct to take them as a self. According to conventions one may say there is a self, but one knows it's not a true self. When it's like this one has seen the Buddha.

This is how Luang Pu Tongrat[22] would teach his disciples. Out walking through the country on one occasion he and some of his monks passed by a couple of water buffaloes. Afterwards he asked the monks, "Did you see those female buffaloes there?" One of his disciples said, "Those weren't females, sir. They were males." So Luang Pu said, "They were females." And the disciple began to argue until he was red in the face. Because he had seen for *sure* that they were males. He saw it with his own eyes. *The teacher is surely mistaken; I'm definitely correct.* He had seen it right for sure.

The disciple let his mindfulness lapse and got more and more entangled in conventions and self until Luang Pu Tongrat said, "Hey! Are there really such things as male and female buffaloes? Who is the one who sees them? Is there a *me*?" He went on asking until the monk regained his mindfulness and realized, *Ohh, the master is teaching the Dhamma. He's leading us to see in terms of ultimate truth that there is no real self. There are no animals or people, no self, no me or them.*

At first we become stuck on the idea of *buffaloes*. And once there are "buffaloes" then there follows, *What sex? What color? How big is it?*—all the time getting more and more deluded. In truth there aren't any of these things. They are all conventions. Ajahn Chah gave the example of a duck and a chicken. Presently we say that a duck goes, "quack, quack" and a chicken goes, "cluck, cluck." But if it happened that they had called ducks "chickens" and chickens "ducks," then presently we would call that which goes "quack, quack" a "chicken" and we'd be calling our chickens "ducks." Our mutual understanding is just based on conventions.

In actuality, it's not correct. These are simply labels which we have come to use when referring to things. But the mind takes these conventions to be real and clings to them as such— that there are animals and people and selves. Attachment is born, which is the cause for the arising of suffering. We need to really investigate this! When you allow the heart to see the truth it can then arrive at emptiness.

Lead the heart to see that everything is empty. The Buddha said, "Mogharāja[23], look on the world as empty and death's king will not be able to find you." Death's king here is dukkha, and if we view the world in this way it won't reach us. Please contemplate this and practice so as to see the conventions and supposition in all material things. These things are impermanent, unsatisfactory and without self, constantly deteriorating and breaking apart.

Like this meditation hall which we've just expanded. It's all finished and ready for use—and it is already breaking down. Since we can't see this yet with our eyes, we need to use our internal eye, the heart. Through contemplating this we can see that these particles of matter have come together temporarily and are deteriorating all the time. Our experiences of feeling, perception, thinking and consciousness arise, remain for a while, and then cease. They're not who we are. For the eye to see objects there must be light. If the eye is functioning, it will receive the reflection of the object. If there is no object, or if there is no light—or if there is an object and light but the vision faculty is impaired—then this won't take place. One will not experience what we call "seeing."

Whether it's seeing, hearing, smelling, tasting or touching, we can observe that these rely on processes that need multiple conditions to take place in order for us to experience them. For one who is blind there is no seeing, for one who is deaf there is no hearing. In other words, the consciousness which would normally arise is obstructed from arising.

Any consciousness that *does* arise simply arises, endures, and then ceases; it doesn't remain long. There is no self there to be found. However, the heart attaches to the "seeing" as *me* seeing. This is where the problem lies. When "I" am the one who hears, then it's: "he insulted *me*," "he criticized *me*," "he doesn't like *me*." That's how the heart will perceive it. So get in and investigate this. *Hey, where is this "me"? Who is the one who sees? Who is the one who hears? Who is the one who smells?* Perceiving this flavor, that bodily sensation, the mental phenomena that arise—they simply arise, remain and then cease. But when the heart goes and becomes attached to them, the sense of self comes up as well. See? This is the way to investigate.

If we find ourselves liking or disliking something then consider: *Is there a self? Is there a "me"? Who is the one who dislikes? Who is the one who loves and hates? Who is angry? Who is scared?* Have a look. One can see into this fact of not-self. If there is enough wisdom present, then we will be able to let go. The mind will be empty. This is tadaṅga vimutti, a momentary liberation, a momentary Nibbāna. This Nibbāna is not far away, ok? It's here in the heart. If we are to see the Dhamma, then we will see Nibbāna in the heart. Awakening to the Dhamma, one awakens right here in the heart.

SET ON NIBBĀNA

Perhaps we have been to India and Nepal to pay homage to the Buddha. With this comes the arising of faith and devotion, of rapture (*pīti*) and happiness (*sukha*). But we still need to use the insight of *vipassanā* to reflect: *This is where the Perfectly Self-Awakened Buddha attained Nibbāna. And the way he attained Nibbāna was by seeing that body and mind are not-self.*

At first there is the appearance of rapture and happiness—this is an aspect of *samatha* practice. When we contemplate until the mind unifies and sees that body and mind are not-self—this is the arising of vipassanā. But in order for the insight of vipassanā to arise we need to rely on samatha, making the mind firmly concentrated. Therefore we need to try and train the mind in becoming calm.

One can watch the in-and-out breath, or use a meditation word like "Bud-dho," or else it is possible to establish mindfulness by internally reciting a chant one is familiar with. The more times one cycles through the chant the firmer it will become. Finally, after remaining with the meditation object for a quite a while, one will feel the mind drop down to merge with "Buddho." Rapture arises at this point, and it's enough to stay with "Buddho." There's no need to focus on the breath. Once rapture and calm come about, the Buddha taught to develop vipassanā, reflecting that: *Buddho means "the one who knows, the one who is awake, the one who is joyful." What did the Buddha know? What had He awoken from? Why was He joyful? Knowing, He knew that body and mind are not-self. He had awoken from upādāna, deluded clinging and attachment. And when there are no more defilements then the heart is joyful.*

So frequently try to contemplate in this way. But if the investigation doesn't bring clear seeing then it's essential to let the mind settle first in a state of concentration. We support this by relying on the five precepts as the heart's foundation. Our conduct will thus be virtuous and pleasing to others. We perform acts of giving as a normal part of our life. We care for our precepts as a normal part of our life. We develop meditation, giving rise to mindfulness and firm concentration. This is the path of practice that will lead one to see the Dhamma. When this path unifies, it will be able to destroy personality view (*sakkāya-diṭṭhi*), skeptical doubt (*vicikicchā*) and attachment to rituals and practices (*sīlabata-parāmāsa*)[24].

This attaining to *Sotāpanna* (stream-entry) isn't something difficult. We just need to understand that all things in this world are conventions. There's no self in any of it. This is how it is for a Sotāpanna. One's faith in the Buddha's dispensation will be absolutely firm. There will be effort to reach the end of suffering. One will have seen that the entire world is an illusion and that all forms of worldly happiness are inauthentic and unstable.

It was like this for Sāriputta and Mahā-Moggallāna[25] prior to their going forth. They had gone to watch the festivities performed at Mount Gijjhakuta, celebrations which could go on for a month, as was the tradition in India at that time. There was great merry-making with everyone dressed up and beautifully ornamented. Sāriputta and Mahā-Moggallāna each led a retinue of 500 young men, and they all went together to enjoy the festivities. But when the fruits of their past good karma reached full maturity, these two friends became disenchanted. The shows and entertainment now appeared boring and wearisome. There was only degeneration and the inevitability of death. After reflecting in this way, these two venerable ones decided to seek the Dhamma as a means to transcend suffering. In the end they both attained to the highest stage of enlightenment.

So let's all reflect on this. These types of happiness and amusement are not permanent or reliable. When this bodily formation experiences the anguish of degeneration and death, these amusements won't be able to help us. We can't simply amuse ourselves in this world, for dukkha—namely ageing, sickness and death—awaits us in the future. It is great pain and suffering.

Our lives are heading for death with each passing mind moment. At all times, with every fraction of a second, we are forever moving closer, facing the arrival of ageing, sickness and death. Reflecting on this will give rise to disenchantment and dispassion for the world.

We should all conduct ourselves heedfully. Endeavor to cultivate the pāramīs. Practice a lot. Even if we have much work and little time, still we must try to look after our mindfulness throughout the day. Continually applying ourselves to contemplating the Dhamma will bring about both tranquility and wisdom. It will allow us to see that our life is uncertain, that death is certain. When this is plainly seen the heart will become weary and dispassionate. It will be set on Nibbāna, freedom from the suffering of endless birth and death.

Investigate so as to arrive at emptiness. If you can see this emptiness clearly just once, you will directly understand the teachings of the Buddha. The heart will be filled with tremendous happiness and you will know that the highest happiness is that of Nibbāna. There is no other happiness which can equal it. When the heart attains to that level of emptiness...oh, the rapture and happiness that appears is overwhelming. If you were to compare it with the happiness found out in the world, this is much more. It is something lasting, something that endures.

BEYOND DOUBT, BEYOND SELF

To practice Dhamma we must look to the present. Because the nature of our thinking is to spin off into matters of past and future. We can spend a lot of time thinking about how to get the best of everything.

This can move into the practice as well. We want to know which meditation subject is best suited to our particular temperament. There are 40 subjects of meditation, and we assume that if we can find the right one our practice will progress quickly. But when we think in this way it leads to doubting and indecision, searching for the most suitable method for our character. At times we may use *Buddho* while walking or sitting meditation and not achieve much tranquility. So we wonder, *Is this right for me? Am I doing it correctly? Maybe I should use a different meditation subject...*

These are simply thoughts of doubt, which is an obstruction to one-pointedness of mind. The more we find ourself doubting and wavering—back-and-forth, *what should I do?*—the more we need to contemplate in a way that brings about an experience of emptiness.

If you try to use an object like *Buddho* while you are caught in doubt, it will just lead to further doubting whether it's the right practice for you. So you don't need to think about anything at all—just let it all be seen in the light of emptiness. Usually when a thought arises in the mind, the habit is to proliferate and build it up further. Seeing everything as *suññatā*—empty—will stop the mind from proliferating. The perception of emptiness is therefore the most suitable meditation subject for those who tend towards doubt.

Whether practicing walking or sitting meditation, we try to contemplate in a way that brings a sense of emptiness to the mind. Investigate the moods and mental impressions that appear and then let them go. There's nothing to them, only arising, existing, ceasing; arising, existing, ceasing. So we practice letting go and not-attaching. Ok? Just let go. It's not appropriate to hold on to them or carry them around. Just observe their arising, existing and ceasing.

This is a teaching of Ajahn Chah's which I've always really appreciated. I've read it so many times—I really like it. He said, "When doubt arises, simply know it as it arises, exists and then ceases." We think this point over, but once we've applied it, doubt returns again. *Hey... if I don't question the teachings, how can I be sure they're correct?* This doubting mind leads us around in circles until we can't handle it anymore.

Alright then, we think. *Time to look for another way.* We then go back to the texts to find a new approach. When we look to the books we're looking for a way out of this delusion. But the fact is, this delusion is right here within us. Aha! If we can know delusion as it arises, exists and ceases, then we'll see through it.

Our natural instinct is to see the *me* and *mine* in all this, to see it as a fixed self or soul. But when we see everything in terms of self, this is what we call a *puthujjana*, an unenlightened being. This is how we normally are, caught up in a sense of *myself*, a sense of *me* and *them*.

Or otherwise, after seeing the sense of self as something frantic and confused, sometimes practitioners get the idea that they can simply flat out reject it. They try to reject the sense of self, deciding that they would be better off without it. Please let me explain what I mean.

"Rejecting" means not wishing to get involved with matters of self. One relies on a peaceful state of mental absorption (*jhāna*) to escape from the suffering associated with the experience of self. When the factors of concentration gather together, one enters into the stillness of deep jhāna and loses all interest in the world outside. Before reaching enlightenment, the Buddha trained in this meditation until skilled at entering the highest level of jhāna. But even after mastering jhāna, the Buddha still hadn't found what He was after. The path which would take Him beyond suffering still had not been found.

On one extreme, there is attaching to the sense of self as something real and stable. On the other extreme, there is completely rejecting the sense of self. Neither of these is the correct path. There is no attempt to understand how the "self" arises, and so both approaches are bound up with delusion.

But the Buddha found another way: seeing through the sense of self and letting it go. Relinquishing attachment. This was different from the two extremes. He investigated until he understood that suffering arises from attachment, dependent upon the misunderstanding that there is a real self. This is seeing that the "self" is "not-self." At this point He was able to let go, putting down the sense of self and attaining to Nibbāna.

All our life we've been building up this idea of a self—of *our*self—and then one day a wise teacher says, "There isn't really any self." And we are able to believe this. But we still can't give it up. It's because the amount of mindfulness and inner tranquility is still not enough to arrive at insight. So we have to keep working at it, keep walking and sitting meditation. After recharging the mind through concentration, get in and investigate. Look to see how the body is just something impermanent, unsatisfactory and not-self and you will see the Dhamma. It's not far away at all. It's right here.

We have to start investigating. *Which bit is me?* Put the teeth in one pile: *are these me?* Put the hair in another pile: *is this me?* Pile up the bones: *are these me?* There's no self there. These things never claimed to be ours. If the mind is calm we can clearly see this. *Ohh, it isn't really mine. There really isn't any self there after all.*

So then why do we attach to these things? We see them as ours, as something attractive and pleasing. But this isn't sane. Though the body is impermanent, we think of it as permanent. Though it's filled with suffering, we think of it as filled with happiness. The body is not ours, but we say that it is; it isn't something beautiful, but we see it that way. This is a form of insanity.

If we keep at the practice it will dawn on us that the body really isn't something beautiful; it really isn't a being or a person or a self. What it really is is a mass of stress and suffering, a mass of impersonality. When we arrive at this insight our heart will arrive at the Dhamma.

In the beginning, though, there is still this sense of self, of me and them. So we bring up mindfulness and investigate. There is no need to doubt the path of practice, although forbidding such doubt from occuring isn't easy to do.

This used to happen to me. When I was newly ordained, I had a lot of doubts about the way of practice. I wanted to get results *quickly*. I wanted to find the direct path, the shortcut. I wanted Ajahn Chah to tell me the straightest way to practice. Oh, I was really in a hurry to get results.

But Ajahn Chah had loving kindness for his disciples. If he had known of a shortcut he would have told us already, for like the Buddha, Ajahn Chah concealed nothing of the teaching. There was nothing closed off; he taught us all that he knew. He told us that the fast track method <u>does</u> exist…don't try to "do" anything. That's right. Just let go completely.

We don't need to do anything special, ok? If we want to get quick results—just let go. Let go of the body, let go of the mind; don't attach to these things as *me* or *mine*. There's no quicker way than this right here. But can we do it?

Well…maybe we're not yet able to let go completely. Maybe we're still attached. In this case, we have to practice first. Begin with giving and moral discipline, along with developing mindfulness and concentration. The wisdom needed to let go is born from these efforts. We work at cultivating the mind, giving up *having* and *being*, giving up the sense of self, of *me* and *them*. This is the fastest way. If you start to have doubts just put them down for the time being. Doubts are something normal; they arise, exist and cease. Just watch them as they come and go.

But if our contemplation doesn't bear fruit it's because our strength of mind (samādhi) is insufficient. Our mindfulness still isn't in the present all the time. In this case we have to continue training the mind. Really try to stay in the present. Don't get into wondering about the future: *What's going to happen? What am I going to be like? How far am I going to get in the practice?*

It sometimes happens that people are in a hurry to get quick results in the practice. Right? We like things fast and want our spiritual development to progress quickly as well. But the way of practicing Dhamma isn't like doing things out in the world. Progress isn't always linear or predictable. To quickly accomplish our spiritual work externally, we can pay homage to the Buddha in any number of ways. But to bring about spiritual development internally, just let go. The heart is then released.

AJAHN CHAH

Venerable Ajahn Chah Bodhiñāna Thera was born in 1918 in a farming village in Ubon Rachathani province, Northeastern Thailand. He ordained as a novice monk for a brief period in his youth, and at the age of 20, still deeply attracted to monastic life, took full ordination. After following the traditional curriculum of Buddhist studies customary in Thailand at that time, he eventually grew disenchanted. In 1946 he abandoned his studies and took up the austere life of a wandering forest monk. Desiring to find the real essence of the Buddha's teachings, he spent the next eight years roaming throughout the country, staying in desolate jungles, caves and cremation grounds, ideal places for developing mediation.

After many arduous years of travel and practice, Ajahn Chah was invited to settle in a thick forest grove near the village of his birth, known as a place of cobras, tigers and ghosts. The monastery that eventually grew up there came to be known as Wat Nong Pah Pong. The conditions were difficult and the basic living requisites scarce, but Ajahn Chah's simple, direct style of teaching began to attract a large following of monks and laypeople. Despite the myriad hardships, they were willing to endure out of great loyalty for their teacher.

In 1966, Ajahn Sumedho, an American intrigued by the strict monastic discipline and way of life, came

to study under Ajahn Chah. From this time on the number of Western disciples grew, and the first overseas branch monastery of Wat Nong Pah Pong was established in England in 1979. Today, Ajahn Chah's teachings and disciples are dotted across the globe, with additional monasteries in Switzerland, Italy, France, Australia, Germany, New Zealand, Canada and the U.S.A.

In 1981 Ajahn Chah's health began to fail, eventually resulting in the need for an operation on his brain. His condition became progressively worse, and he spent the last ten years of his life bedridden and unable to speak. Throughout this time he was carefully tended by his faithful disciples. On the 16th of January, 1992, Venerable Ajahn Chah passed away at the age of 74, leaving behind a legacy that is still growing today. Headed by the King and Queen of Thailand, his funeral was attended by nearly a million people, paying their last respects to a man who truly embodied the Buddha's teachings.

AJAHN ANAN

Venerable Ajahn Anan Akiñcano was born Anan Chan-in in the provincial town of Saraburi, Central Thailand, on March 31st, 1954. From an early age he would regularly accompany his parents to the local temple to chant and pay respect to the monks, and he recalls experiencing feelings of great ease and joy when looking at images of the Buddha. During his school days he was known to be well-mannered and keen in his studies, and after graduation was hired as an accountant at Siam Cement Company. Though a diligent employee, he found himself increasingly drawn to Buddhist practice and began living at a nearby monastery during his hours away from work.

For the next year, while working full-time and strictly observing the eight precepts of a lay practitioner, he was able to increase his meditation efforts and his confidence in the Buddha's teachings. After offering food to the monks each morning, he would travel to work and then return to the monastery in the evening to practice mediation. One day he had an experience of profound insight into the nature of all phenomena, followed by three days and three nights of a happiness unlike anything he had felt before. This experience removed any remaining doubts about committing his life to the Buddha's teachings and soon afterwards he decided to enter the monastic order.

On July 3rd, 1975, Ajahn Anan took full ordination under his preceptor and teacher, the Venerable Ajahn Chah. He was given the Pāli name Akiñcano, meaning "one without worries," and spent the next four years diligently practicing meditation and developing care and attentiveness around the more routine aspects of monastic life. During this period he acted as Ajahn Chah's personal attendant, which provided him with the opportunity to develop a close connection with his teacher. Though his meditation was up and down during these early years as a monk, in his fourth year it reached a point where it did not decline again.

After this intensive training period with Ajahn Chah, Ajahn Anan was allowed the opportunity to seek out more secluded places to further his efforts in meditation. Living in remote forests and charnel grounds, he met with various hardships both outside and within. He committed himself to this way of life for several years, growing in endurance, contending with serious bouts of malaria which took him close to death on many occasions. In 1984 he was offered a section of uninhabited land on which to build a forest monastery, and along with two other monks and a novice settled in the dense forest of Rayong province at what is now known as Wat Marp Jan, "the forest monastery of the moonlit mountain."

Over 25 years later, Ajahn Anan's reputation as a meditation master has grown, along with the number of monks coming to practice under him and seeking his guidance. Today, he attends to his many duties as abbot and teacher, sharing his time between monks and lay guests and looking after a growing number of branch monasteries. Though by no means comprehensive, the teachings collected in this book represent a portion of the wisdom he has shared over the years.

GLOSSARY

ajahn   Teacher (Thai); used as a title for senior monks.

anattā   Not self, impersonal, without individual essence; one of the three characteristics of all conditioned phenomena.

anger   Any form of aversion or disliking. One of the three primary mental defilements. (Pāli: *dosa*)

anicca   Impermanent, transient, having the nature to arise and pass away; one of the three characteristics of all conditioned phenomena.

arahant   An enlightened being or "worthy one," free from all greed, anger and delusion.

ārammaṇa   A mental impression brought about by contact at any of six sense bases. In the Thai language the word can also refer to an emotion or mood.

avijjā   Fundamental ignorance, that is, ignorance of one's own true nature. Lack of clear insight into the Four Noble Truths.

āyatana   Sense medium, consisting of the internal sense bases (eye, ear, nose, tongue, body, mind) and their respective objects (forms, sounds, smells, tastes, tactile sensations, mind-objects).

body and mind Physical and mental phenomena. Body is identical with the first of the five *khandas* and mind encompasses the remaining four. (Pāli: *nāma-rūpa*)

Buddha	"The Awakened One"; the historical Buddha, Siddhattha Gotama, who taught in northern India in the 6th Century B.C.

Buddha — "The Awakened One"; the historical Buddha, Siddhattha Gotama, who taught in northern India in the 6th Century B.C.

Buddho — (1) Awakened or enlightened awareness; "the one who knows, the one who is awake, the one who is joyful."
(2) A meditation word which, through constant mental repitition, can bring the mind to *samādhi*.

Dhamma — Truth, Reality, Nature, or the laws of nature considered as a whole. The term is often used to refer to the Buddha's teachings as well as to the truth to which they point. (Skt. *Dharma*)

dukkha — Suffering, unsatisfactoriness, discontent; one of the three characteristics of all conditioned phenomena. Literally, "hard to bear."

Eightfold Path — The path of practice composed of eight ideal or perfected qualities of body, speech and mind. These eight qualities can be further divided into the threefold training of *sīla*, *samādhi* and *paññā*. The factors of Right Speech, Right Action and Right Livelihood make up the training in virtue and moral discipline (*sīla*); Right Effort, Right Mindfulness and Right Concentration make up the training of concentration (*samādhi*); while Right View and Right Intention represent the training in wisdom (*paññā*).

eight worldly conditions — Gain and loss, praise and criticism, fame and disrepute, pleasure and pain.

five precepts — The five basic guidelines for training oneself in wholesome actions of body and speech: refraining from killing other beings; refraining from stealing; refraining from sexual misconduct; refraining from lying and false speech; refraining from the use of intoxicants.

four elements	Earth, Water, Fire and Air. The primary qualities of matter. Earth has the characteristic of hardness, water of fluidity and cohesion, fire of heat, and air of motion. All four are present in every material object, though in varying proportions. (Pāli: *dhātu*)
Four Noble Truths	The first teaching of the Buddha: the Truth of Suffering, its origin, its cessation, and the path to the cessation of suffering.
greed	Any form of deluded wanting, desire or attraction. One of the three primary mental defilements. (Pāli: *lobha*)
jhāna	Mental absorption; an advanced state of concentration wherein the mind becomes unified with its meditation subject. A state of *jhāna* arises from the temporary suppresion of the five hindrances through the development of five mental factors: directed thought, evaluation, rapture, happiness, and one-pointedness of mind. The eight levels of *jhāna* consist of four form and four formless, each progressively more refined than the previous one.
karma	Volitional action of body, speech or mind. Cause leading to an effect. (Pāli: *kamma*)
khandha	Aggregate or "heap"; the psychophysical components that the deluded mind attaches to as a self: bodily form, feeling, memory and perception, mental formations, and consciousness. (Skt. *skandha*)
kilesa	Mental defilements; unwholesome qualities that obscure clarity and purity of mind. There are three primary roots: greed, anger and delusion.
lokuttara	Transcendent or supramundane states; "beyond the world."
Luang Pu	(Thai) Venerable grandfather; a reverential term used for very senior monks.

magga-phala	Path and Fruition. Refers to the paths leading to, and the final attainment of, the four stages of enlightenment. That is, the path and fruition of stream-entry (*sotāpanna*), of once-return (*sakadāgāmi*), of non-return (*anāgāmi*) and of full enlightenment (*arahant*). Attainment to the fruition to any of these stages is dependent on abandoning the ten fetters to varying degrees. They are: (1) personality view, (2) skeptical doubt, (3) attachment to rituals and practices, (4) sensual desire, (5) aversion, (6) attachment to form realms, (7) attachment to formless realms, (8) conceit, (9) restlessness, (10) ignorance. The first three fetters are abandoned at the stage of *sotāpanna*, the first level of enlightenment. The fourth and fifth fetters are attenuated at the stage of *sakadāgāmi* and fully abandoned at the stage of *anāgāmi*. The final five fetters are abandoned with the attainment of *arahant*, the final stage of enlightenment.
mindfulness	Awareness, recollection, attentiveness. The ability to keep one's attention deliberately fixed on whatever one chooses to observe. (Pāli: *sati*)
mental hindrances	Five qualities which are obstacles to the mind and blind our mental vision. They are sensual desire, ill-will, dullness, restlessness and skeptical doubt. (Pāli: *nīvaraṇa*)
Nibbāna	Freedom from suffering; the extinguishing of greed, anger and delusion; enlightenment; awakening. The state realized when the heart is freed from the conditions that bind it to conventional reality (see *magga-phala*). The ultimate goal of Buddhist training. (Skt. *Nirvāṇa*)
pāli	The language of the earliest Buddhist scriptures, closely related to Sanskrit.

paṭicca-samuppāda	Dependent origination, conditioned co-arising; one of the central doctrines of the Buddhist teaching. The 12-stage conditioned process which brings about suffering. Founded on the "this/that" principle of specific causality; i.e., when there is *this*, then *that* arises. It proceeds as follows: from ignorance arises karma-formations; from karma-formations, consciousness; from consciousness, mental and physical phenomena; from mental and physical phenomena, the six sense bases; from the six sense bases, contact; from contact, feeling; from feeling, craving; from craving, clinging; from clinging, becoming; from becoming, birth; from birth, old age, death, sorrow, lamentation, pain, grief and despair.
paññā	Wisdom; true understanding of the nature of reality. Insight into impermanence, unsatisfactoriness, and not-self.
pāpa	Wrongdoing, demerit; evil or unwholesome actions.
pāramī	The ten spiritual perfections, consisting of: generosity, moral discipline, renunciation, wisdom, energectic effort, patient endurance, truthfulness, determination, loving kindness and equanimity. Virtues accumulated over many lifetimes manifesting as wholesome dispositions. Can be thought of as one's collective spiritual maturity.
pīti	Rapture; the third factor of absorption.
puñña	Merit. The accumulation of positive karma and the actions which contribute to this; the spiritual power of good deeds.

puthujjana	Worldling, ordinary person. Anyone still possessed of all 10 fetters which bind beings to the rounds of rebirth, and thus yet to attain to the first stage of enlightenment.
pūjā	Honor, respect, homage, worship, devotional observances, devotional offerings.
sakkāya-diṭṭhi	See note 20, pg. 98.
samādhi	Meditative calm and stability. One-pointedness of mind. It refers to both the process of focusing awareness unwaveringly upon a single meditation object and the resultant state of such concentrated attention. Right concentration (or *Sammā Samādhi*) is the eigth factor of the Noble Eightfold Path.
samatha	The development of tranquil states of mind.
samutti	Conventional, dualistic, or nominal reality; the reality of names, suppositions and determinations. For instance, a cup is not intrinsically a cup; it is only determined to be so.
saṁsāra	The round of existence, "perpetual wandering"; the ongoing cycle of birth and death. The unenlightened, unsatisfactory experience of life.
sangha	In general, the community of those who practice the Buddhist path; on a deeper level, anyone who has attained one of the eight stages of enlightenment.
saṅkhāra	Conditioned phenomena; that which is created from the coming together of various conditions. Although by definition *saṅkhāra* includes both physical and mental phenomena, it can also be used to refer to the fourth of the five aggregates, i.e. thoughts, moods and mental states.

sīla	Virtue, morality, ethical conduct. Also refers to the specific moral precepts taken on by Buddhist laypersons, novices, monks and nuns.
sotāpanna	Stream-entry. The first stage of enlightenment which is reached upon the abandonment of the first three fetters. One who has reached this stage will have unshakeable faith in the Buddha, Dhamma and Sangha, and is incapable of breaking the five moral precepts. One will be reborn seven more times at most, and not in a state lower than the human realm.
sukha	Happiness, pleasure, joy, bliss; one of the three feelings; the fourth factor of absorption.
tadaṅga-vimutti	Temporary liberation of the heart through insight into impermanence, suffering and not-self; however, the liberating insight has not yet reached a level of attainment.
taṇhā	Desire or craving conditioned by delusion. Includes *kāma taṇhā*, craving for sensual pleasure; *bhava taṇhā*, craving for being or experiencing; *vibhava taṇhā*, craving for not-being or not-experiencing. The Second Noble Truth states that *taṇhā* is the cause of suffering and should be abandoned.
three characteristics	Impermanence (*anicca*), unsatisfactoriness (*dukkha*), and not-self (*anattā*). The qualities of impermanence and unsatisfactoriness apply only to those phenomena which arise from causes and conditions. (Pāli: *ti-lakkhaṇa*)
upādāna	Clinging, grasping, attachment. The four kinds of clinging are: clinging to sensual pleasure, clinging to views, clinging to rituals and practices and clinging to the personality-belief.

vedanā	Feeling: pleasant, unpleasant and neutral, which can be either bodily or mental.
vimutti	Freedom, liberation (see *Nibbāna*).
vipassanā	Clear-seeing; insight into *anicca*, *dukkha*, *anattā*, and the methods of contemplation or investigation that lead to such profound knowledge.
wat	(Thai) Buddhist monastery.

NOTES

1   Aligned with the half and full moons, these are days on which members of the lay community will come to the monastery in order to take moral precepts, engage in chanting, listen to Dhamma talks, and practice sitting and walking meditation.

2   A famous teaching given by the Buddha to a spontaneous gathering of 1,250 of his enlightened disciples at the Bamboo Grove, near Rajagaha, on the full moon of February. The occasion is celebrated by the annual festival of Māgha Pūjā. This discourse, the "Ovādapāṭimokkha," forms verses 183-185 of the *Dhammapada*.

3   Awakened or enlightened; "the one who knows, one who is awake, one who is joyful." A traditional epithet of the Buddha. Also used as a meditation word in the Thai Forest Tradition.

4   The fourth of the Noble Truths taught by the Buddha; the eightfold path of practice leading to the cessation of *dukkha*, consisting of Right View, Right Intention, Right Speech, Right Action, Right Livelihood, Right Effort, Right Mindfulness, and Right Concentration.

5   Even in the present day, one can still find cremation grounds in Thailand where dead bodies are left overnight out in the open for several days. Monks will often seek out these quiet, lonely locations as a place to practice meditation and challenge any latent fears of death, ghosts or other spirits.

6   The threefold training (*sīla, samādhi* and *paññā*); a condensed representation of the Noble Eightfold Path.

7   See glossary (*magga-phala*).

8   This second view is reflective of the Brahmin caste system which still exists in India today.

9   In Buddhist cosmology, the 31 levels of existence can be
      further divided into three worlds: the sensual, form and
      formless. Deities, humans and below are part of the the
      sensual world, while the form and formless worlds are made
      up of brahma gods.

10   Realms of gods. The 20 highest realms of existence within
      the 31 levels of Buddhist cosmology.

11   Venerable Ajahn Kinaree Jantiyo. Prominent Thai forest
      meditation master. One of Ajahn Chah's early teachers.

12   Three important factors in the process of dependent origi-
      nation, causing suffering and bondage to the cycle of birth
      and death.

13   Refers to the attainment of a stage of enlightenment. See
      glossary (*magga-phala*).

14   The forest monastery in Northeast Thailand founded by
      Venerable Ajahn Chah.

15   As this was given in the free-form style of a spoken discourse,
      both here, and later in the talk, Ajahn Anan explains only
      part of the process of dependent origination. For a complete
      summary of the 12-stage conditioned process, see glossary
      (*paṭiccasamuppāda).*

16   The five ascetics who followed Siddhattha Gotama when
      he was cultivating ascetic practices prior to his Enlighten-
      ment. They left him when he renounced extreme asceticism
      for the Middle Way, though later became the Buddha's first
      disciples.

17   The five *khanda*s (aggregates, groups) of form, feeling,
      perception, mental formations and consciousness are that
      which comprise the psycho-physical experience known as
      the "self." Form is what is is commonly referred to as "body,"
      while the remaining four khandas make up what we call
      "mind."

18   This is a play on words in the Thai language. Seeing "the
      true self," in this instance has the meaning of insight into
      Truth, Dhamma.

19   Perfect One; literally, the one who has "thus gone" or "thus come." Traditional epithet usually reserved solely for the Buddha.

20   Self-identity view; the view that a true self exists. This is abandoned completely only on the attainment of the first stage of Enlightenment. There are four basic types of self-identity view: that the true self is (1) identical with, (2) contained within, (3) independent of, or (4) the owner of any of the five *khanda*s (see note 17, above).

21   To "enter the stream of *Nibbāna*" is to reach the first stage of enlightenment. One who has reached this stage has a maximum of seven lives remaining until full enlightenment and will never again be reborn into the lower realms (animal, ghost, demon and hell realms).

22   Venerable Ajahn Tongrat Kantasīlo. Another of Ajahn Chah's early teachers.

23   A religious seeker who took his questions to the Buddha and attained to enlightenment upon hearing the Buddha's answer.

24   These are the three fetters abandoned by a practitioner in attaining to the stage of stream-entry (*sotāpanna*). See glossary (*magga-phala*).

25   The two chief disciples of the Buddha. Venerable Sāriputta was declared by the Buddha to be foremost in wisdom; Venerable Mahā-Moggallāna was declared foremost in psychic powers.

ALSO BY AJAHN ANAN

Available for download at www.watmarpjan.org

Seeking Buddho (Book)
Four Dhamma talks, from the basics of meditation to the more intensive levels of practice.

Simple Teachings on Higher Truths (Book)
Compiled teachings of Ajahn Anan, gradually progressing from the basic to the profound.

Sotāpattimagga: the Path of the Sotāpanna (Book)
Ajahn Anan's detailed exposition on the direct path of practice towards stream-entry.

Australia (MP3 Talks)
Talks given on Ajahn Anan's trip to Bodhivana Monastery, Melbourne and Bodhikusuma Buddhist Meditation Centre, Sydney in 2011.

Acariyadhamma (MP3 Talks)
Talks on a variety of topics from the mundane to the supramundane. Translated by Ajahn Kalyano.

Samadhi Bhavana (30 min VCD)
Basic meditation instructions, illustrating all the how-tos of sitting and walking meditation in an easy-to-follow format.

Unbounded Mind (MP3 Talks)
Collection of translated talks given to various Western monks.

The Dhamma of Ajahn Anan Akiñcano (MP3 Talks)
Formal talks and Q&A's addressing a variety of everyday issues. Translated by Ajahn Kalyano.